ATTRACTING MONEY

ACHIEVING FINANCIAL PROSPERITY IN THE MODERN WORLD

Hi ,

My name is Deviana sharon S,the author,content editor,content strategist, from india,but live in the US,and i dedicate this website to the ascended masters,saint germain,lady portia,angels,devas,fairies &animal totems that have helped me in my journey to ascension in this lifetime balancig 51%negative karma in 25 years and fulfilling my full and highest divine plan and potential,Dharma(soul purpose),RIGHTFUL DUTY, and karma to make my ascension with my twin flame berkeley in this lifetime a retired US military veteran Seargeant and broadcasting journalism degree pursuer,BA final year and a writer by trade,similar age to me. I am a Author,publisher,artcle/content editor ,content strategist and Publish books and ebooks,bookseller.im also a business owner ,founder&director of sharon&berkeley real estate investments LLP india,also owning the brand and shopify store of Sharon&berkeley Excellence doing th right thing advantage of the witch&the raven and this website/store,and have a BA in psychology from minot state university with philosophy minor&broadcasting concentration.

A persons fortune is changed
through the mind a persons mind
is changed through the power of
repetition

By Deviana Sharon seelam

Terms and Conditions

LEGAL NOTICE

The Publisher has strived to be as exact and finish as conceivable in the formation of this report, despite the way that he doesn't warrant or speak to whenever that the substance inside are precise because of the quickly changing nature of the Internet.

While all endeavors have been made to confirm data gave in this distribution, the Publisher accepts no accountability for mistakes, oversights, or opposite translation of the topic thus. Any apparent insults of explicit people, people groups, or associations are accidental.

In reasonable exhortation books, similar to whatever else throughout everyday life, there are no assurances of pay made. Perusers are forewarned to answer on their own judgment about their individual conditions to act in like manner.

This book isn't planned for use as a wellspring of legitimate, business, bookkeeping or monetary counsel. All perusers are informed to look for administrations with respect to able experts in lawful, business, bookkeeping and money fields.

You are urged to print this book for simple perusing

Table Of Contents

Foreword

In this book you'll find the establishments of the sign cycle and the inbuilt force of your brain to deliver whatever reality you like. You'll jump into the investigation of your mindfulness and find that it's among the most fantastic and energizing spaces one may occupy. Welcome to the unending possibility that is you! Everything in your life is an outcome of what you comprehend, what you experience and how you connect with your mindfulness. These components make up the natural source from which all the other things creates. Finding out about yourself might be the most charming undertaking one may envision. Showing is a force of cognizance at the inward level, and isn't dictated by any external conditions. We as a whole offer the equivalent inside source; nobody gets pretty much. The sole distinction is that a couple of people are more discerning of it than others. Yet, with this and with an ideal demeanor to learn, you can go as profoundly as you need. This is your readiness to investigate the obscure.

The more you comprehend about the obscure the more you truly grasp how little you comprehend. It makes you humble and takes you back to the area of marvels, supernatural occurrences and enchantment. A space in which everything is possible.

It would be ideal if you study this book with a totally receptive outlook. You don't need to believe all that is composed here – essentially investigate as a researcher would do. At the point when you hit a section that is difficult to get a handle on, enjoy a reprieve and consider it for a little while. Allow your psyche to handle this new data. Peruse this digital book two or multiple times, take as much time as is needed and produce your own encounters

CHAPTER 1

The importance of Recognizing

Rundown

Most people never consider what they wish in their lives. They live without this information or deliberation and become casualties of their own condition. Work is basically about a work – to

make do monetarily. Life turns into a progression of difficulties like deciding to live somewhere in light of the fact that the lease is reasonable,

never acknowledging how to be seeing someone or turning out to be

You Have To See It

Inside you there's a wanting more. Is it importance, contact or a more extravagant comprehension of life? Nobody has ever familiar such people with the idea of interminable chance. "As a man thinketh, so is he." A significant mode to showing the existence you wish is to thoroughly consider what you wish out of life. Would could it be that you wish to do with your life? An extraordinary exercise is to take a piece of paper and put down the responses to the going with questions:

What is my most profound need?

What might I want to accomplish in the course of my life?

What might I want to accomplish this year? Where might I wish to be in five years? Where might I wish to be in twenty years? What am I incredible at?

Look into all fields of your life:

Your profession

Your connections

Your health

Your monetary situation

How you have a great time (how you spend your excursions)

After you've put down top notch of what you wish to accomplish in your life, you'll need to set needs for them. Essentially take the rundown that you put down and give each subject 1 - 5 focuses. 1 turning into the most un-significant

truly essential that you're in enthusiastic harmony with your objectives – they need to feel right to you. In the event that you just make objectives in your psyche that are not valuable to you then you'll find yourself struggling attempting to achieve them.

What happens with most people situation is that they've an objective that feels right for them, at that point they start working at their objective. Put in an unexpected way, they place their consideration into making their objective a reality. A little while pass by and nothing happens. Presently alarm kicks in and the objective for reasons unknown seems inaccessible, the inspiration is down to nada.

This is where you need to feel your disappointment. Don't just place it away or markdown it – face it as absolutely and deliberately as you can. This might be upsetting for you anyway it will assist you with getting your objective. How is this? At the point when you wish to modify your existence you clearly need to accomplish something uniquely in contrast to what you've done beforehand.

So this is the place where reality check comes in. You glance around and can't perceive any change. In any case, changes may have just occurred in your reasoning and lead. You may have put matters into action that you can't yet see. Disappointment sets in when you assume that issues should happen sooner than you're prepared for them. Keep in mind – there are no ridiculous objectives, just unreasonable time spans.

So feel your disappointment and let it resolve. View what you've done and realign your techniques. On the off chance that single direction doesn't prompt achievement don't stop by then – simply endeavor another. In the event that you stay with an objective you'll achieve it.

- 10 - Occasionally you may push too hard when you just need to give up and ease the heat off. You question yourself now, trusting there's nothing you can accomplish. Go to the spot in your mind where you realize you can't bomb. Perusing a book or review an inspirational film may assist with getting you realigned with your powerful source.

CHAPTER 2-

WHAT DO YOU HAVE TO OFFER

Synopsis

Most successful individuals have something in common. They enjoy what they do. You won't discover wealthy and successful individuals that detest what they do.

Gifts

Every one of us is unmatched, having specific abilities and blessings. It's something inherently implicit in every last one of us, a compounding of energy designs driving toward a characteristic family relationship for specific issues throughout everyday life, specific methods of being. Among the most vital positions in your day to day existence is to find these abilities and endowments inside yourself, which is an

affirmation of what you've brought into your creation.

How about we assume that you're introduced a sledge without having any cognizance of how to utilize this apparatus. Stay with me now – this is an unmistakable misrepresentation of a profoundly critical part of your fact. You're introduced nails however you use the mistaken finish of the sledge. You can't perceive any accomplishment with accomplishing your undertaking of beating in the nails. You've the device yet not the comprehension of its right use. Similarly, how may we deal with our lives without understanding the numerous devices usable and their applications? You may even have a moment of edified lucidity. We may all identify with finally understanding something that had been wrecking us. Wouldn't it be pleasant in the event that someone had shared the basic information ahead of time – prior to experiencing disappointment and possibly give up?

Understanding your own qualities and gifts is totally essential for any further advances you take throughout everyday life. Putting them down should make them

all the more genuine to you in case you're not used to considering them. On the off chance that you comprehend your unmistakable qualities and endowments you should have the option to record them in several sentences without pondering the method. In case you're not sure, or you genuinely have no

sign, here are a few clues that will assist you with portraying them:

Recollect your youth:

What were the toys you gotten a kick out of the chance to play with?

⁻ What were you captivated with?

⊓ What did you like most to play?

What presents did you need to get for your birthday and Christmas?

⊓ What did you seek to become in your future?

Ask your closest associates:

Advise your associates that you wish to reconsider your gifts and you need a sensible assessment from them. Make sure to request that your associates be 100% honest with you. Allow them to investigate you and request that they clear out the thing you're doing expertly – keep it on an individual plane.

⊐ What do your colleagues accept you're acceptable at?

⁻ What do they accept your abilities are?

What do they ask you should do with your life?

Ask yourself several inquiries

Take a journal and read through these enquiries. Verify you open your brain and let these inquiries harden in your creative mind. Try not to take these inquiries too truly, play with them and in like manner put down what sways up suddenly – these are incidentally the most major answers.

These inquiries are arranged to rescue your awareness once again from the ordinary attitude. The most reliable arrangements are constantly found external the typical area of reasoning. Keep in mind, your brain is important for the aggregate mindfulness; thusly you've admittance to all data. Your psyche is associated with the boundless wellspring of all universe.

☐ What might you do in the event that you had enough pay not to work until kingdom come?

What were your aspirations when you were more youthful?

What do you accept is outlandish for you to achieve?

⊔ What might you do in the event that you obtained 5 million dollars?

_ What might you do if this was the break of destruction?

☐ What might you do on the off chance that you were unable to bomb?

⁻ What are your claims to fame and abilities?

Do you have a need yet don't have the foggiest idea how to fulfill it?

What do you like most about others?

What might your optimal way of life resemble?

What does achievement mean for you?

What makes you genuinely upbeat?

What does an ideal day look like for you?

What might you do if there were no impediments?

What might you be regarded and perceived for?

Where do you see your life in 10 years?

If you were eternal, what might you achieve with your life?

What requirements to move to make this a superior Earth?

What are you glad for?

What might you want to accomplish this year?

☐ What might you do any other way in the event that you could start by and by? Finding your qualities and gifts resembles first building the cellar for your home. It's your establishment. It resembles the earth from which a strong and delightful tree may develop. It supplies you with your one of a kind potential. It's the remarkable enrichment that accompanied you when you were conceived. You are being asked here to support it till it's generous enough to manage you in your life.

Use the blessings you came in with or the ones you obtained en route. You may turn out to be great at something however you'll never find valid, enduring joy with it on the off chance that you can't claim it completely.

Use whatever devices you feel comfortable with. Endeavor to find an approach to delve further into yourself. This is your life – and you're justified, despite any trouble!

Try not to blow your time pursuing another person's aspiration or objective or anything that isn't given to you that you can't guarantee first as your own.

CHAPTER 3-
THINGS SHOULDN'T
HOLD YOU BACK OR
DOWN

Synopsis

At a certain point in the course of your life, you may wonder why others are so fruitful with cash when you're definitely not.

Contingent on how intently you look, you'll have a ton of answers.

What's Stopping You

Do these sound like something you think?

☐ They're simply more prosperous than I am

☐ They've preferred preparing over I do

☐ They were naturally introduced to a well off family

☐ They're white and have more advantageous chances than I do

☐ They previously had the income to start a business

☐ They previously had the income to put resources into realty

⊔ They're more brilliant than I am

☐ They're more youthful than I am

¯ They look in a way that is better than I do

They probably work more enthusiastically than I do

The rundown probably continues filling numerous pages. Cash is the subject that delivers the most thoughts, trailed by the issue of connections.

You probably won't get this yet, yet your ideas are the example for your existence. On the off chance that you realized that, would you designedly make one from the rundown above? Likely not, as these thoughts are not strong by any means. These convictions produce a fact that leaves you 'playing' the hoodwink, and besides, keeps you right where you are. You're not bettering your life the slightest bit. For what reason would we say we are delivering these thoughts in any case, when we comprehend that they're not useful at all? The appropriate response stays nature of our cognizance. The vast majority of us were told

that there's a universe out there and this universe conditions our fact. It's the normal thought that life happens to us. The majority of us get these ideas upheld a few times each day. The outcome is that our awareness becomes engraved each day with a similar message. The message with the normal, worn out idea.

Meanwhile, as adults, we're not even aware that our life, 'as it happens' is built around an idea. It turns into a major reality that we demonstrate to ourselves in each second.

So how would we escape this problem? We need to make a stride in reverse and view our ideas. Take a piece of paper and a pencil and put down all the thoughts you have about pay. Try not to think exorbitantly, be unconstrained. At the point when you've run out of your own thoughts, consider what others ideas are about cash.

At that point mark every thought with an 'I' or an 'S' depending if the idea is preventing or strong. Ruining thoughts don't uphold creating abundance, steady ideas do. Presently, see your rundown and check each steady and frustrating thought. What is your score? What number of thwarting ideas do you have, and what number of steady thoughts do you have?

Perceive that all the preventing thoughts don't uphold the creation of fortune. Presently, take a new piece of paper, and conceptualize ideas that will unequivocally create the abundance you'd prefer to have. At the point when you're finished with the rundown, look at every one of your new thoughts and produce a psychological picture. Hold this picture for in any event ten - twenty seconds. You may require some training, however each time you do it, you'll improve at it. Do this activity in a quiet, serene and loosened up climate, as this will assist with dazzling these thoughts into your cognizance.

Keep in mind, thoughts are the plan of what will show in your life. With a little planning, you'll have the option to move onto the following stage, which is feeling your ideas. Feel like these new thoughts, that encourage what you genuinely need to make, have truly been showed.

How can it feel to be a mogul?

How can it feel to have abundance in your life?

⊔ How can it feel to have more pay than you can spend?

⊔ How can it feel to provide for others?

⊓ How can it feel to buy something without review the cost?

At whatever point you see yourself thinking or talking an upsetting conviction about cash, quit what you're doing. Re-visitation of the spot in your psyche where you call up one of your intentionally made convictions about income, and associate with it. The more you achieve this, the more you'll prepare your mind to think in a new manner, a way that heads to carrying on with a plentiful and great life.

CHAPTER 4-

GREAT MOTIVES.

Synopsis

Goal alludes to what one intends to do or achieve. Expectation just means a strategy that one intends to follow: it's my aim to take an occasion one month from now. So you may state your tending is accused of an attitude that coordinates *itself toward accomplishing something*

Mean It Into Your Life

We should get into that one day you stir in the first part of the day and you don't have any expectations. What might happen? Totally nothing – you probably would remain in bed till you expected to eat something or you may have to go to the washroom. That implies that some external conditions, perhaps the biologic techniques – which are, all things considered, substantial points – make you move. Without aim you'd accomplish nothing, not even the merest assignment.

You probably won't be mindful of your goals as you find yourself getting up and up naturally, as you 'wish' or 'need' to go to work. So a couple of your aims are abandoning you being perceptive of them.

Notwithstanding, in the present condition we're examining purposeful expectations. You emerge up and you think and consider what you'd prefer to accomplish now. You think about your objectives throughout everyday life and plan to make them happen. Proceeding with your goals is a truly dynamic cycle that gives your life a course. By changing and realigning your aims you'll achieve your objectives and achieve your fantasies.

Is masterminding an objective equivalent to holding an expectation?

They're comparative, however not the equivalent. You can mastermind the same number of objectives as you require, in any case, in the event that you don't have a mean to achieve any of them – they'll never happen. An aim is significantly more

powerful than just defining an objective throughout everyday life. Aims will leave you achieve any objective. An objective is a subject; it's something that is happening later on. An expectation incorporates this and adds a driving capacity to it. This driving force is always in the present and will decide the result of your activity.

Step by step instructions to show up at powerful aims.

We use aim to manage our consideration a new way to deliver a new or distinctive truth. For example, maybe you'd prefer to change your occupation. Most people start with the goal of having a superior occupation,

s the bygone one isn't fulfilling any more. However, inconvenience may be blending here as of now . . .

On the off chance that you go on from something you don't care to something you favor, you may keep your present status from getting undertakings. To make effective expectations, it's critical to manage the present status of issues first, while doing some scientific considering everything. Over once more, the key is to assume full liability, and to grasp that you're the solitary individual liable for the current conditions.

Kill any decisions of your present site, till you can see it from an unbiased position. There was a point in your life when it was the absolute choice. Try not to contrast the present time and place and your past, as you've since had new encounters and acquired a more refined viewpoint that extra involvement with this space brings. This is an essential mistake in reasoning; it resembles a proviso in the cerebrum. You hop starting with one course of events then onto the next timetable, and afterward liken the two. This prompts counterfeit ends. Leave the past behind – don't reexamine it!

Innovative reasoning is never a reaction from an earlier time; it's eternity an imaginative demonstration in the present. On the off chance that you see your present spot without judgment, you're ready to see and dissect your life history. Just from a nonpartisan perspective may you settle on a strong new choice. This new choice will be founded on determined purpose as opposed to responding to situation. This is the place where decision and caution come in.

From the situation of being unbiased, you can ask yourself the going with inquiries:

⊔ What do I appreciate about my present occupation?

⊔ What improve in my next occupation?

⊔ What might be the absolute occupation for me?

☐ What might I want to feel from my next occupation?

☐ What am I extraordinary at?

☐ In which locales is this occupation supporting me to live my full possibility?

Put down the responses to these enquiries, and start to work out a few full sentences dependent on your answers. Incorporate all the positive subtleties. Make these sentences as exact as could be expected under the circumstances. A representation explanation may peruse something like this: "My next occupation is empowering; it streams with me, makes me happy, and I'm ready to take in and develop from it.

At the point when you're done, perused it so anyone might hear. In the event that you've inconvenience saying the sentence, or in any event, remembering it, at that point it isn't prepared. Just take two or three minutes and calibrate it.

Aims are formed in your cognizant psyche; in any case, it's your inner mind that gets these orders and makes the basic chances in your day to day existence. Put in an unexpected way, your cognizant brain chooses this new chance – delivering a new reality.

☐ Utilize just positive words

⊓ Include a time span

⊩ Get freed of refutations

⊔ Be exact

Here's a simple test. Try not to think about a blue elephant! What happened? You thought about the blue elephant, you may have even envisioned it. The psyche doesn't work systematically. It can't appreciate words like 'don't' or 'not.' It works generally in pictures, sounds, and smells. You wish to dodge the usage of any negative words in your goals. Everlastingly build up your aims so that they resonate the result of what you'd prefer to create.

Representation of how not to do it:

I don't wish to have such a lot of obligation. More gainful outline:

In my new occupation I feel comfortable with my obligations.

There's a distinction between creating in your own universe and delivering in the actual world. At the point when you produce inside yourself there's no time influenced – your awareness is ageless! For example, in the event that you'd prefer to adjust your demeanor toward your chief, you don't need to set a time span. You can simply make the goal: "I esteem my chief," or, "I esteem my manager's perspectives and impressions." It will work immediately if there's no other thought or aim in its manner.

At the point when you address the actual world, setting a time period gets pivotal. The actual world works inside reality. In the event that you build another home, first you've an arrangement, and afterward you move soil, set up wood, set up pipes and move furniture till the house is finished. It requires some investment and work. So on the off chance that you cause your expectation yet you to prohibit the time period – your aim becomes being referred to. For example: "I'm working in my fantasy occupation." Well, you'd without a doubt say quickly: "I'm not!" It sounds more like a certification than a goal. Incorporate the time period, and this outline transforms into: "I'm working in my fantasy occupation, a half year from now."

Focus on any reactions you have when you manufacture your expectation. Your brain may meddle and advise you: "No chance, I'll never procure this," or "this is unfathomable." If you experience these brief instant decisions, manufacture your goals in an unexpected way, so they feel more attainable.

At times you should break a gigantic aim into humbler pieces. For example: "In about fourteen days I'm a tycoon," is an aim that probably won't work for most people. In any case, a goal like: "day by day I have more pay to spend," might get you there sooner than you envision.

CHAPTER 5-STEPS TO BRINGING WEALTH

Synopsis

Let me the opening shot by conceding that I've been dirt poor already. I've had those occasions where I was out and out worried over how I planned to take care of the tabs that were truly past due! I've in like manner had times where I've had above and beyond pay to take care of every one of my tabs and buy boats, automobiles and take enormous occasions. I've had both of the encounters very quickly.

I will clarify, actually essentially, how I've dealt with return into arrangement with delivering a very sizable amount of income&more

Trust It

Adhere to a meaningful boundary in the sand. Show up at a decision. From right now forward you'll attract more income and produce a structure and propensities that help a new and bettered level of abundance. You need to represent this. You must be hungry for change.

You need to believe you can do this. Regardless of whether you're scared that this time won't be not quite the same as different occasions, you've made this choice. You'll make a couple of moves now that won't neglect you out the back passageway on yourself. Require a touch of exertion presently to move yourself in the bigger objective.

What is it decisively that you wish to appear as something else? On the off chance that you wish more income to come in the entryway, what amount and how habitually? Do you wish an extra 10,000 this year or month to month? Do you wish your business to net an extra million or net an extra million? When? This month? This year? By one year from now? You need to choose or it gets one of those "sometime in the not so distant future" things.

On the off chance that, a sum feels inaccessible, at that point make it more diminutive. In the event that the sum you've chosen feels close to nothing you'll actually be wishing you had more income, than make it bigger. Most importantly, whatever amount of cash you're choosing to have, mean what you state. This is so natural, yet this is the place where most people fall and the rest their endeavors don't produce victories.

Furthermore, something extra, its no one else's business what numbers you pick. A few people may pass judgment on your numbers as being pretty much nothing or enormous dependent on their own life. However long you feel firm about your determination and you're not whimping out on yourself, go on it!

What will you spend the cash on? Again, this is your cash and you must be genuinely appended to it. Where is it going to go? In case you will pay obligations, show up at an arrangement for how you'll achieve it and afterward pick where the cash will go when the obligation is repaid. Presently you've the sources of an arrangement. That was straightforward, eh?!

In case you will save pay, what amount and to where? You may need to do a touch of envisioning and enquiry to consummate this progression. In the event that you wish to extend your business with a portion of this extra cash, it may take you some additional arranging, yet you'll be extremely empowered. This thrill will help move you towards progress.

Presently, clear up and put down how this will feel once accomplished. I perceive to a couple of you this progression will seem like a waste. Try not to skirt this progression. You need to make this objective so genuine in your cerebrum and heart that you run, not stroll, to more wealth. This progression is basic in both method and the Law of Attraction.

Produce exact activities and propensities that you'll apply starting presently to help this objective of more wealth. You may just require several activities. This isn't advanced science. For a couple of you, it may just involve creating responsibility. You as of now comprehend what to do. For a couple of you, it very well may be tied in with creating a whole new relationship with pay.

I know two or three you need to leave your place of employment or eliminate or add new colleagues. Truly, you may fear a couple of things on your rundown, however will you be happy once you do it? On the off chance that the appropriate response is definitely, keep it on your rundown. Analyze enormous activities into little advances so they're absorbable.

Propelled activity. Large numbers of you've heard this multiple times however you're as yet not holding a candle to the current situation it. It is safe to say that you are making moves that vibe incredible? Are they another person's "should's" or are they truly something you've chosen to do. Your instinct is addressing you. It is safe to say that you are hearing?

Who will uphold you? Is it accurate to say that you are contributed enough to own this objective? Will you accept that you'll succeed in any event, when you don't accept there are any indications of improvement throughout quite a while period? Who will help you in a manner that truly works for you? Consistency is critical.

On the off chance that you really wish to have more cash in your ledger and wallet, at that point print this out and follow the means in the following 24 hours. This entire cycle may take as meager as an hour or two.

How energetic would you say you are tied in with getting affluent? It is anything but a matter of "in the event that" you'll be more prosperous, yet "when."

Wrapping Up

We should unite all that you've learned. Comprehend that satisfying your aspirations is the motivation behind your life. It's practicing your qualities and blessings to add to the better great of all. Comprehend that satisfying your fantasies is your destiny. Never at any point allow anyone to remove this intense power from you.

Choose what you wish throughout everyday life. This may change during your life, so survey your objectives and aspirations like clockwork. Line up with your since quite a while ago run objectives and adjust your short-run objectives.

Comprehend your qualities, blessings and abilities. In like manner comprehend your frail zones, practice your qualities and get help from others for your feeble territories. Have you thought about a coach?

Understand that you've limitless consideration. Choose where you wish to set your consideration. Breaking point the districts where you squander your consideration. Increment the zones where you wish results.

Use your creative mind. Envision what it seems like to have achieved your objectives. Imagine what it seems like when you live your aspirations.

Contemplate your convictions. Your convictions produce reality. Substitute non-supporting convictions with convictions that affirm your objectives and desire. Art strong goals that express your life desire.

Fathom that what you hold in your cognizance attracts like conditions in your day to day existence.